GW00786467

Series 584

A Ladybird Book

Series 584

A Ladybird Book

COMMERCIAL VEHICLES

by DAVID CAREY

Publishers: Ladybird Books Ltd . Loughborough
© Ladybird Books Ltd (formerly Wills & Hepworth Ltd) 1969
Printed in England

Fiat 241

The Fiat company of Italy produce this good-looking light truck with two-seater forward control cab and dropside body. A complete heating and- ventilating system is provided in the cab. The body will carry a load of 27½ cwt. Unusual in commercial vehicle design is the independent coil-spring front suspension.

Manufacturer: Fiat S.p.A., Turin, Italy. *Engine:* Petrol, 4-cylinder, 1438 c.c. capacity, developing 55 horse-power (metric). *Overall length:* 15 feet $2\frac{13}{64}$ inches. *Gross vehicle weight:* $2\frac{3}{4}$ tons.

Ford Transit

The Transit range consists of several alternative models from 12 cwt. to 35 cwt. carrying capacity and fitted with different types of body. The van shown opposite will carry 30 cwt. and has 28 cubic feet of load space. The normal control cab is entered by sliding doors. Double rear wheels are fitted.

Manufacturer: The Ford Motor Company Ltd., Dagenham, Essex. *Engine:* Petrol, V4-cylinder, 1996 c.c. capacity, developing 80.5 brake horse-power. *Overall length:* 16 feet 11 inches. *Gross vehicle weight:* 2.99 tons.

4

7214 0187 2

BMC 350 EA Van

This van is designed as a big box body on wheels and has a maximum load space of 322 cubic feet. Smaller than normal road wheels reduce the loading height of the floor and there is a choice of hinged or sliding doors for the forward control cab. The engine is tilted at 55 degrees.

Manufacturer: Austin/Morris Division, British Leyland Motor Corporation, Longbridge, Birmingham. *Engines:* Petrol, 4-cylinder, 2520 c.c. capacity, developing 70 brake horse-power; diesel, 4-cylinder, 2520 c.c. capacity, developing 66 brake horse-power. *Overall length:* 15 feet 11 inches. *Gross vehicle weight:* 3.5 tons.

BMC 360 WF Truck

Built at the Bathgate (Scotland) factory of BLMC, the 360 WF is a normal control truck for general contract and delivery duties. It is supplied only as a chassis/cab unit to which almost any type of body can later be fitted by the owner. These vehicles are particularly suitable for overseas use.

Manufacturer: Truck & Bus Division, British Leyland Motor Corporation, Bathgate, Scotland. *Engines:* Petrol, 6-cylinder, 3993 c.c. capacity, developing 87 brake horse-power; diesel, 4-cylinder, 3800 c.c. capacity, developing 68 brake horse-power. *Chassis length:* 17 feet $9\frac{7}{8}$ inches. *Gross vehicle weight:* 3.6 tons.

Land-Rover, 4-wheel Drive, Forward Control

The largest model in the famous Land-Rover range, the Forward Control is designed to carry loads across rough country where ordinary trucks cannot go. It is very strong and the drive can be taken by the two rear wheels only or by all four wheels at once.

Manufacturer: The Rover Company Ltd., Solihull, Warwickshire. *Engine:* Petrol, 6-cylinder, 2625 c.c. capacity, developing 88 brake horse-power. 4-cylinder petrol or diesel engines also available. *Overall length:* 16 feet 1 inch. *Gross vehicle weight:* 3.7 tons.

BMC 360 FG Truck

This is the forward control version of the BLMC light truck range. The cab has many special features, including low scuttle windows through which the driver and his mate can see the kerb. The driving seat is adjustable for height and the doors are cut back to reduce projection beyond the width of the vehicle.

Manufacturer: British Leyland Motor Corporation, Bathgate, Scotland. *Engines:* Petrol, 4-cylinder, 2199 c.c. capacity, developing 70 brake horse-power; diesel, 4-cylinder, 2178 c.c. capacity, developing 58 brake horse-power. *Overall length:* 16 feet 8 inches. *Gross vehicle weight:* 3.6 tons.

Commer KA.40 'Walk-Thru'

The Commer Walk-Thru chassis are very suitable for use as mobile shops and they are operated by grocers, butchers, fishmongers, bakers and the like in various parts of the country. The bodies are specially built by Smith's Delivery Vehicles Ltd. in Gateshead-on-Tyne. A grocer's mobile shop is shown opposite.

Manufacturer: Commer Cars Limited, Luton, Bedfordshire. *Engines:* Petrol, 4-cylinder, 2266 c.c. capacity, developing 56 brake horse-power; diesel, 4-cylinder, 2611 c.c. capacity, developing 60 brake horse-power. *Overall length:* 20 feet. *Gross vehicle weight:* $4\frac{1}{2}$ tons.

Ford D Series 200

The Ford D range contains vehicles from 5.1 tons to 20 tons gross vehicle weight (GVW). The 200 is the smallest. The chassis is constructed to take specialised types of bodywork and the comfortable three-seater forward control cab can be tilted forward so that the engine can be easily attended to.

Manufacturer: Ford Motor Company Ltd., Dagenham, Essex. *Engine:* Diesel, 4-cylinder, 3968 c.c. capacity, developing 82.5 brake horse-power. *Chassis length:* 19 feet 1 inch. *Gross vehicle weight:* 5.1 tons.

Bedford J2S Tipper

Seen everywhere on road repair work and highway and construction duties, the Bedford J2S tipper is a popular vehicle with contractors and municipal authorities. The normal control cab and frontal design are typical of the Bedford JS series of models which range up to the J6S with a gross vehicle weight of 10.75 tons.

Manufacturer: Vauxhall Motors Ltd., Luton, Bedfordshire. *Engines:* Petrol, 6-cylinder, 3519 c.c. capacity, developing 100 brake horse-power; diesel, 4-cylinder, 3614 c.c. capacity, developing 70 brake horse-power. *Chassis length:* 16 feet 1 inch. *Gross vehicle weight:* 6 tons.

Commer VC 4

Four basic models are included in the Commer V series. There is also a choice of four wheelbase lengths to meet tipper and haulage requirements, two petrol and two diesel engine alternatives and four gearboxes offering four, five or six speeds. These are all forward control models with the same overall cab design. The smallest model is illustrated.

Manufacturer: Commer Cars Ltd., Dunstable, Bedfordshire. *Engines:* Petrol, 6-cylinder, 4139 c.c. capacity, developing 107 brake horse-power; diesel, 4-cylinder, 3860 c.c. capacity, developing 80 brake horse-power. *Chassis length:* 21 feet 2 inches. *Gross vehicle weight:* 7.8 tons.

BMC 700 FM

This is one of BMC's medium weight trucks for general haulage work. It is mainly supplied in chassis form for the fitting of specialised bodies, but standard platform and dropside bodies can be fitted. The forward control cab has the BMC low-level windows, and a rather unusual front end design.

Manufacturer: British Leyland Motor Corporation, Bathgate, Scotland. *Engine:* Diesel, 4-cylinder, 3800 c.c. capacity, developing 76 brake horse-power. *Chassis length:* 20 feet $6\frac{1}{16}$ inches. *Gross vehicle weight:* 7 tons.

Ford D300 'Baby-Artic'

Here is the first-ever matched tractor/trailer unit produced by separate companies. The tractor is by Ford and the semi-trailer by the Hands company. The combination, which will carry a 6-ton load, is lighter and smaller than most articulated vehicles and is useful for getting in and out of confined spaces.

Manufacturer: Ford Motor Company Ltd., Dagenham, Essex. *Engine:* Diesel, 4-cylinder, 3968 c.c. capacity, developing 82.5 brake horse-power. *Chassis length:* 11 feet 9 inches. *Gross combination weight:* (GCW) 10 tons.

WALTER THORKE LTD VIVI FOOD DISTRIBUTORS

FORD

MKE 346E

Dodge 500 Series Low Loader

Stop-start delivery work needs a vehicle that is easy to load and unload. The Dodge Low Loader is built for this type of operation and has a chassis frame height of only 25 inches (laden). The cab gives good visibility and has a low step for easy getting in and out.

Manufacturer: Dodge Brothers (Britain) Ltd., Kew, Surrey. *Engine:* Diesel, Chrysler V6-cylinder, 5770 c.c. capacity, developing 130 brake horse-power. *Chassis length:* 22 feet 2¾ inches. *Gross vehicle weight:* 10.27 tons.

Bedford RSH 4x4

One of a great many Bedford models, the RSH is a four-wheel drive cross-country tipper built for work on rough building sites and other difficult off-the-road situations. The cab and front-end styling are easily distinguishable from other types of Bedford trucks.

Manufacturer: Vauxhall Motors Ltd., Luton, Bedfordshire. *Engines:* Petrol, 6-cylinder, 4927 c.c. capacity, developing 133 brake horse-power; diesel, 6-cylinder, 5420 c.c. capacity, developing 107 brake horse-power. *Wheelbase:* 11 feet. *Gross vehicle weight:* 10.30 tons.

BMC Laird LR1160

The trucks in the 'Laird' range are among the newest BMC medium-weight commercials and the LR1160 is one of five basic models. The forward control cab has a de luxe specification, including fully-adjustable driving seat, padded dash and door panels, door pockets, heater and plenty of window area all round.

Manufacturer: British Leyland Motor Corporation, Bathgate, Scotland. *Engine:* Diesel, 6-cylinder, 5655 c.c. capacity, developing 105 brake horse-power. *Chassis length:* 22 feet 1¼ inches. *Gross vehicle weight:* 11.6 tons.

Dennis Refuse Collector

Dennis chassis fitted with special bodies are used a great deal by municipal authorities all over the country. In particular, the Refuse Collector can be seen operating in many towns. The body takes about 24 cubic yards of refuse which is compressed into a tightly-packed mass by a hydraulic ram. The cab holds the driver and five loaders.

Manufacturer: Dennis Bros. Ltd., Guildford, Surrey. *Engine:* Perkins diesel, 6-cylinder, 5805 c.c. capacity, developing 120 brake horse-power. *Overall length:* 24 feet 2 inches. *Gross vehicle weight:* 11.75 tons.

Albion Chieftain Super 6

Designed as a high-quality medium-weight range of vehicles, the Chieftain Super 6 series includes four haulage models, three tippers, and a tractor for articulated vehicle operation. A 5-speed gearbox is standard equipment, with options of 6, 9 or 10 speeds for easy, long-distance running.

Manufacturer: Albion Motors Ltd., Glasgow, Scotland. *Engine:* Leyland diesel, 6-cylinder, 6075 c.c. capacity, developing 106 brake horse-power. *Chassis length:* 19 feet 5 inches to 26 feet 10 inches according to model. *Gross vehicle weight:* 12.5 tons.

Bedford TK Truck

Here is one of the Bedford heavy-duty trucks with a load-carrying capacity of about 8 tons. Our picture shows the vehicle with factory-built dropside body. The forward control cab is well forward of the engine and there is a wide shelf behind the driver's and passenger's seats.

Manufacturer: Vauxhall Motors Ltd., Luton, Bedford-shire. *Engine:* Diesel, 6-cylinder, 6243 c.c. capacity, developing 124 brake horse-power. *Overall length:* (Standard body) 24 feet 8½ inches. *Gross vehicle weight:* 12.5 tons.

Commer C Range

Built and powered to carry medium-weight loads over long haulage distances, the trucks of the Commer C range have a forward control cab and a 5-speed synchromesh gearbox. Overdrive is available as an optional extra and when fitted provides a sixth, or high cruising gear. There is a choice of four wheelbase lengths from 9 feet 7 inches to 15 feet 7 inches.

Manufacturer: Commer Cars Ltd., Dunstable, Bedfordshire. *Engine:* Rootes diesel, 3-cylinder two-stroke, 3520 c.c. capacity, developing 135 brake horse-power. *Gross vehicle weight:* 13 tons.

Seddon Diesel 13-Four

This is the smallest in a series of Seddon trucks that ranges up to three-axle tanker trailers with a gross combination weight of 32 tons. The cab is of the forward control type with a distinctive appearance and large windscreen area. Our picture opposite shows a special concrete mixer on the tipper chassis.

Manufacturer: Seddon Motors Limited, Oldham, Lancashire. *Engine:* Perkins diesel, 6-cylinder, 5806 c.c. capacity, developing 120 brake horse-power. *Mixer capacity:* 4/5 cubic yards. *Gross vehicle weight:* 14 tons.

Fiat 643 N

Another truck from Fiat, the 643 is a long-distance haulage vehicle. The cab is interesting in that the passenger's seat has armrests and a headrest, and there is provision for the fitting of two bunks between the seats and the cab back. The driver's seat is fully adjustable.

Manufacturer: Fiat S.p.A., Turin, Italy. *Engine:* Diesel, 6-cylinder, 9161 c.c. capacity, developing 160 horse-power (metric). *Overall length:* 24 feet 6 inches. *Gross vehicle weight:* 12.85 tons. *Towing capacity:* 14 tons.

Thornycroft Nubian Crash Tender

The Thornycroft Nubian has been developed into a high-performance cross-country chassis which is widely used for fire/crash tenders. These vehicles are stationed on civil and military airfields all over the world. They can also be used for oil-prospecting, surveying, pest control and heavy recovery duties in difficult areas.

Manufacturer: Transport Equipment (Thornycroft) Ltd., Basingstoke, Hampshire. *Engine:* Rolls-Royce petrol, 8-cylinder, 6522 c.c. capacity, developing 197 brake horse-power. *Chassis length:* 20 feet $3\frac{5}{8}$ inches. *Gross vehicle weight:* 14 tons.

Bedford KM Series

This is Bedford's heavy duty series with trucks, tippers and tractors ranging from 14 tons gross vehicle weight to 24 tons gross train weight (GTW). The truck shown opposite is rated at 16 tons. The cab is of forward control design, similar to the TK models, and has access doors to the engine on either side.

Manufacturer: Vauxhall Motors Ltd., Luton, Bedfordshire. *Engine:* Diesel, 6-cylinder, 7634 c.c. capacity, developing 143 brake horse-power. *Wheelbase:* 13 feet 2 inches. *Gross vehicle weight:* 16 tons.

Dennis Pax V Tipper

Dennis vehicles are widely used for various municipal duties like refuse collecting, drain emptying, etc., but they are operated on general-purpose work as well. The Pax V tipper is a little unusual in that the cab is made of glass fibre, fire-resistant, reinforced plastic. Steel is the more traditional material.

Manufacturer: Dennis Bros. Ltd., Guildford, Surrey. *Engine:* Diesel, 6-cylinder, 5805 c.c. capacity, developing 120 brake horse-power. *Body capacity:* 8 cubic yards. *Gross vehicle weight:* 15 tons.

ERF Two-axle Rigid

The ERF two-axle rigid chassis are built for hard work and heavy loads, and are suitable for medium or long haulage distances. The vehicles look tough and impressive, with a forward control cab that gives good driver visibility through the wide and deep windscreen. This is another cab built of glass fibre.

Manufacturer: E.R.F. Limited, Sandbach, Cheshire. *Engine:* Perkins diesel, 6-cylinder, 5800 c.c. capacity, developing 120 brake horse-power. (Other engines are also available). *Overall length:* 25 feet 11$\frac{5}{8}$ inches. *Gross vehicle weight:* 16 tons.

Guy 'Big J4' 4-wheel Load Carrier

Guy Big J4 trucks are in a fairly popular group of medium-weight vehicles which can be used for medium to long distance transport. The cab follows the modern trend, giving a high degree of comfort for driver and mate and offering such conveniences as windscreen washers and four-headlamp lighting as standard equipment.

Manufacturer: Guy Motors Ltd., Wolverhampton. *Engines:* Leyland diesel, 6-cylinder, 6540 c.c. capacity, developing 138 brake horse-power; AEC diesel, 6-cylinder, 8189 c.c. capacity, developing 149 brake horse-power. *Wheelbase:* 12 feet 1 inch. *Gross vehicle weight:* 16 tons.

AEC Mercury

Another of the good quality, tough, middle-weight vehicles, the AEC Mercury is ideal for motorway operation, long distance hauls and tipper work. The all-steel forward control cab can be tilted forward for engine accessibility and has car-type heating, with ample ventilation. A choice of wheelbases and other equipment is available.

Manufacturer: A.E.C. Limited, Southall, Middlesex. *Engine:* Diesel, 6-cylinder, 8189 c.c. capacity, developing 151 brake horse-power. *Wheelbase:* 10 feet 9 inches. *Gross vehicle weight:* 16 tons.

Ford D1000 Tipper

The Ford D1000 series is powered by Ford's turbo-charged diesel engine. Turbo-design provides increased intake of air into the engine for greater efficiency, better fuel economy and quieter operation among other advantages. Our illustration shows a D1000 metal-bodied tipper with forward control cab. Note the radiator guard to save front-end damage.

Manufacturer: Ford Motor Company Ltd., Dagenham, Essex. *Engine:* Diesel, 6-cylinder turbocharged, 5904 c.c. capacity, developing 150 brake horse-power. *Wheelbase:* Choice of lengths. *Gross vehicle weight:* 16 tons.

Mercedes-Benz LP 1920

A handsome vehicle from Germany is this Mercedes truck. The engine is mounted under the floor of the forward control cab which does not therefore have the usual big hump in the middle. Vehicles of this type are sometimes seen in Britain but visitors to the Continent will meet them frequently.

Manufacturer: Daimler-Benz Aktiengesellschaft, Mannheim, Germany. *Engine:* Diesel, 6-cylinder, 10809 c.c. capacity, developing 230 brake horse-power. *Chassis length:* 28 feet (approx.). *Gross vehicle weight:* 19 tons.

Albion Super Reiver 20

Albion produce a three-axle, six-wheeled haulage and tipper chassis, with four double driving wheels at the rear. It has a 5-speed gearbox with a sixth over-drive speed for more economical cruising. The spacious cab gives excellent all-round visibility and has been specially designed to reduce driver fatigue.

Manufacturer: Albion Motors Ltd., Glasgow, Scotland. *Engine:* Leyland diesel, 6-cylinder, 6444 c.c. capacity, developing 125 brake horse-power. *Overall length:* (Standard body) 27 feet 7 inches. *Gross vehicle weight:* 20 tons.

Magirus-Deutz 6x6 Dumper

A rugged and interesting vehicle is this Magirus dumper from West Germany. It has drive from all six wheels, hence the 6x6 reference, and is powered by an air-cooled diesel engine which requires no cooling water. The tipping body has a capacity of nearly 9 cubic yards. A normal control cab is provided.

Manufacturer: Klöckner-Humboldt-Deutz AG, Ulm, West Germany. *Engine:* Air-cooled diesel, V6-cylinder, 8730 c.c. capacity, developing 156 brake horse-power. *Overall length:* 22 feet $11\frac{9}{16}$ inches. *Gross vehicle weight:* 20 tons.

Foden

With this Foden truck we move into the heavyweight division of commercial vehicles. The picture opposite shows a special body for carrying sand, ballast or coal fitted to the 8-wheeler chassis. The vehicle is capable of carrying up to a 16-ton load. A 12-speed gearbox is fitted and there is a choice of four engines.

Manufacturer: Fodens Limited, Sandbach, Cheshire. *Engine:* Diesel, 6-cylinder supercharged, 4800 c.c. capacity, developing 180 brake horse-power. (Other engines available.) *Overall length:* 30 feet (approx.). *Gross vehicle weight:* 24 tons.

Volvo FB888

This is one of Sweden's heavyweight commercials designed for national or international haulage. It has an 8-speed gearbox and four separate braking systems for safety. Cab equipment is very complete and includes a rest bunk behind the seats. A trailer can be towed behind the vehicle, providing a high overall load capacity.

Manufacturer: AB Volvo, Goteborg, Sweden. *Engine:* Diesel, 6-cylinder, 9600 c.c. capacity, developing 270 brake horse-power. *Chassis length:* 30 feet $3\frac{3}{4}$ inches. *Gross vehicle weight:* 21.6 tons.

Seddon Diesel 16-Four Tractor

The Seddon 16-Four is a tractor unit for use with a variety of trailer types. The cab, similar in appearance to the 13-Four cab illustrated on page 23, provides good driver and passenger comfort with heating and ventilating systems and plenty of visibility. An illuminated roof panel is available as an optional extra.

Manufacturer: Seddon Motors Ltd., Oldham, Lancashire. *Engine:* Diesel, V8-cylinder, 8360 c.c. capacity, developing 170 brake horse-power. *Chassis length:* 16 feet $5\frac{1}{2}$ inches. *Gross combination weight:* 26 tons.

Scammell Routeman

An 8-wheeler chassis designed specifically for heavy and difficult tipping work, the Routeman has drive from both rear axles, or double drive as it is called. All four front wheels are used for steering, which gives this large vehicle surprisingly good manoeuvring powers. A sound-proofed, glass fibre cab is fitted.

Manufacturer: Scammell Lorries Ltd., Watford, Hertfordshire. *Engine:* Leyland diesel, 6-cylinder, 11100 c.c. capacity, developing 185 brake horse-power. *Chassis length:* 29 feet 9 inches. *Gross vehicle weight:* 24 tons.

Scania LBS 110H

A two-seater cab of impressive appearance is a feature of this Swedish-built vehicle. The 6-wheel chassis can be used either with a separate truck body, in which case it can tow a trailer as well, or as a tractor for operation with an articulated semi-trailer.

Manufacturer: AB Scania-Vabis, Sodertalje, Sweden. *Engine:* Diesel, 6-cylinder turbocharged, 11037 c.c. capacity, developing 256 brake horse-power. *Chassis length:* Various chassis available. *Gross vehicle weight:* 22 tons approx.

ERF Four-axle Rigid

As with the two-axle model described on page 28, the cab of this commercial is made of non-corrosive glass fibre and offers excellent driver/passenger accommodation. This type of vehicle is constructed of the best quality materials and designed for heavy, long-distance haulage. Double or single rear axle drives are available.

Manufacturer: E.R.F. Limited, Sandbach, Cheshire. *Engine:* Gardner diesel, 6-cylinder, 10450 c.c. capacity, developing 150 brake horse-power. (Other engine alternatives are available.) *Chassis length:* 30 feet. *Gross vehicle weight:* 24 tons.

AEC Mammoth Major

This is another four-axle rigid chassis, designed as a 28-ton gross weight truck but legally permitted to operate at 24 to 26 tons in the United Kingdom. Like all commercial vehicles it can be operated with any one of a variety of bodies depending on the kind of loads to be carried.

Manufacturer: A.E.C. Limited, Southall, Middlesex. *Engine:* Diesel, 6-cylinder, 11310 c.c. capacity, developing 187 brake horse-power. *Chassis length:* 25 feet $10\frac{1}{2}$ inches to 35 feet $11\frac{1}{2}$ inches depending on model. *Gross vehicle weight:* 24/26 tons.

Leyland Octopus

The four-axle Leyland Freightline Octopus range includes heavy-duty, high-performance haulage and tipper models with a choice of engines, 5, 6 or 7-speed gearbox and single or double rear axle drive. A very comfortable cab is provided giving excellent visibility, and single or double sleeping bunks are available for overseas operators.

Manufacturer: Leyland Motors Limited, Leyland, Lancashire. *Engine:* Diesel, 6-cylinder, 11100 c.c. capacity, developing 200 brake horse-power. *Chassis length:* 35 feet 9 inches (maximum). *Gross vehicle weight:* 26 tons (32 tons GCW with trailer).

Guy 'Big J8'

Here we have another tough 8-wheel truck for heavy loads and long-distance transport. Frontal treatment conforms to the modern flat design and the forward driving position ensures that driver and passenger are able to see all round. Single or double drive is offered as well as a choice of engines and gearboxes.

Manufacturer: Guy Motors Limited, Wolverhampton. *Engines:* A range of seven 6-cylinder diesel engines is available, developing from 149 to 192 brake horse-power. *Chassis length:* 29 feet $10\frac{1}{2}$ inches (maximum). *Gross vehicle weight:* 24 tons (32 tons GCW with trailer).

Atkinson Silver Knight Tractor

Like most of the tractor units in use today, this Atkinson 6-wheel tractor can be detached from its trailer and used to pull other freight whilst the trailer is being loaded or unloaded. It is very suitable for long-distance haulage carrying loads of around 24 tons.

Manufacturer: Atkinsons Vehicles Ltd., Preston, Lancashire. *Engine:* Diesel: 6-cylinder, 12170 c.c. capacity, developing 212 brake horse-power. *Tractor length:* 18 feet 3½ inches (other chassis available). *Gross vehicle weight:* 32 tons.

Leyland Gas Turbine Tractor

Possibly the most advanced truck chassis in the world, the Leyland gas turbine tractor is designed to run at speeds of up to 70 miles per hour. The engine is a development of the famous Rover gas turbine car engine and has an expected life before overhaul of about 500,000 miles. Transmission is by 5-speed fully-automatic gearbox.

Manufacturer: British Leyland Motor Corporation Ltd., Leyland, Lancashire. *Engine:* Gas turbine, developing 350/400 horse-power and operating at around 30,000 revolutions per minute. *Chassis length:* 20 feet 1 inch. *Gross train weight:* 38 tons.

Scammell 4x4 Mountaineer

A really tough, powerful, go-anywhere truck or tractor, the Mountaineer is built for work in the rugged areas of the world, such as oil fields and big construction sites. This four-wheel drive monster looks slightly old-fashioned when compared with more normal commercials, but its operating performance is anything but old-fashioned.

Manufacturer: Scammell Lorries Ltd., Watford, Hertfordshire. *Engine:* Leyland diesel, 6-cylinder, 11100 c.c. capacity, developing 150 brake horse-power. (Several other engines are available.) *Wheelbase:* 19 feet. *Gross train weight:* 60 tons.

Foden Dump Truck

From the illustration opposite it is obvious that the Foden dump truck is another vehicle built for a tough life. It will carry a load of 24 tons and has a body capacity of 20½ cubic yards. Note the unusual half-cab on one side of the engine and the wide-section rear tyres.

Manufacturer: Fodens Limited, Sandbach, Cheshire. *Engine:* Diesel, 6-cylinder supercharged, 4800 c.c. capacity, developing 180 brake horse-power. *Overall length:* 24 feet 2 inches. *Gross vehicle weight:* 34.5 tons.

Leyland Super Hippo

British commercial vehicles, particularly the really heavy-duty ones, are in great demand in overseas countries where there are fewer restrictions on size, weight and speed. The Leyland Super Hippo models are normally-controlled 6-wheeled vehicles designed primarily for overseas operation. They can be used with or without a trailer.

Manufacturer: Leyland Motors Ltd., Leyland, Lancashire. *Engine:* Diesel, 6-cylinder, 11100 c.c. capacity, developing 200 brake horse-power. *Chassis length:* 30 feet. *Gross train weight:* 48 tons.

ERF Three-axle Tractor

In this modern world, wherever there is a heavy load there is a vehicle capable of hauling it. The ERF special duty tractor is just such a vehicle. The tractor itself has six wheels while the trailer, in this case, has a further six double wheels. The cab is of forward control design and fibre glass construction.

Manufacturer: E.R.F. Limited, Sandbach, Cheshire. *Engine:* Rolls-Royce diesel, 6-cylinder turbocharged, 12170 c.c. capacity, developing 260 brake horse-power. *Gross train weight:* Up to 130 tons.

Thornycroft 'Mighty Antar' Tractor

An enormous tractor capable of pulling a payload of 90 tons, the Mighty Antar is the biggest single transport unit built in Britain. It is widely used overseas especially in the Middle East where heavy oilfield equipment has to be moved. It will travel at a speed of 30 miles per hour fully laden.

Manufacturer: Transport Equipment (Thornycroft) Ltd., Basingstoke, Hampshire. *Engine:* Rolls-Royce diesel, 8-cylinder supercharged, 16200 c.c. capacity, developing 365 brake horse-power. *Gross train weight:* Up to 150 tons.

Scammell 6x6 Super Constructor

The Scammell 6-wheel drive Super Constructor tractor is capable of hauling very big loads by itself, but when coupled with one or two other tractors the towing capacity becomes quite amazing. Our picture shows a 180-ton casting being pulled by a Super Contractor and pushed by a second tractor coupled behind the load-carrying trailer.

Manufacturer: Scammell Lorries Ltd., Watford, Hertfordshire. *Engine:* Diesel, 6-cylinder, 11100 c.c. capacity, developing 200 brake horse-power. (Alternative power units are available.) *Chassis length:* 25 feet 3¾ inches. *Gross train weight:* Up to 250 tons.

INDEX TO COMMERCIAL VEHICLES